The Life & Fate Of A Harassment Victim

The Life & Fate Of A Harassment Victim

Edward T. Evans, Ph, D.

THE LIFE & FATE OF A HARASSMENT VICTIM

iUniverse books may be ordered through booksellers or by contacting:

iUniverse
1663 Liberty Drive
Bloomington, IN 47403
www.iuniverse.com
844-349-9409

ISBN: 978-1-6632-5672-0 (sc)
ISBN: 978-1-6632-5669-0 (e)

Library of Congress Control Number: 2023918575

Print information available on the last page.

iUniverse rev. date: 10/31/2023

Chapter 1

I was a child, and he was a boy
But our trouble was one and the same.
I sought the answer to the question "Why?"
He followed his cross in vain.

Beauty and truth we cherished in life
And together our friendship grew.
Companionship changed and turned into love,
A love that is known by few.

All that we asked was to be left alone
Our happiness was full and free.
But a meaning in life brings on envy and strife
And society would not let us be.

Time has a way of healing a wound,
but our trouble is again the same
I seek the answer to the question "Why?"
He follows his cross in vain.

And that's the way it was. Danny, the neighborhood boy was a high school senior. He took me into a nearby woods, while the rest of the kids played depression kick-the-can. How could six year-old Eddie know that the game big Danny wanted to play was evil, and that his father would not want him to play? You see, it was 1936 and children mostly played outside. So a routine developed; when the weather was good, Eddie and Danny had two games for fun: kick-the-can and evil in the woods.

For some reason Danny liked to smooch. Well, so did I. After school we often went to our basement for a long session. Maybe boys don't do that in your book, but we sure had a good time at it. All that stopped, when Danny went to Jail for maleficence.

Chapter 2

Before the jail term, my mother was delighted with the friendship I had with Danny. She was determined to let her children enjoy things she couldn't when she was young. She wanted her children to have lots of friends. She had a Sunday school class and lived for activities with the neighborhood children. This attitude pleased Danny, but my country-raised mother was naïve. Although she couldn't see the obvious, she was something special. Her desire to help others was a religion.

One day as she was hanging curtains. She noticed a large round face practically glued to her dining room window. When she went out to see who it was, her mother rushed over and explained that the face was her daughter Doris and she had downs syndrome. She was just inquisitive about her new neighbor. She explained that Doris was mentally handicapped and nobody in the neighborhood would invite her in to their house. Well, Mother turned that around. Mother let her come over whenever she chose. Also, when my older brother Johnny was born, Doris chose to play cowboys and Indians with him. Her big pink under panties captured many an Indian. Then when I came along, Doris was allowed to play house with me. Yes, anything feminine was quite appealing to me. Mother thought that was a sweet part of my nature. Was she ever right! Then when my little brother Timmy was born, Doris played every game imaginable with him and his friends.

There were vacations of course. Mother was determined that we would get to know America. So in the summer we either traveled West or East. Out at Jane's beautiful cabin up in Colorado Springs, we had pancakes with wild berries and then on to Yellowstone and Old Faithful, which then really did erupt every fifteen minutes. When we traveled east to see early America, we visited Washington's church in Alexandria and I got to sit in his church pew. It was so exciting.

Chapter 3

High School was a completely different experience. There wasn't time for any foolishness. I had play practice after school. Yes, Miss Strickler, the drama teacher thought I had talent and put me in the lead of each school play for four years. Many students hated me, but I didn't care. I had a lot of fun being under the spotlight. I starred in "The Flying Adams" in and "Foot loose" in 1946. Then "The Little Prince" and "Football Player" in 1947. In the "Football Player" there was a scene where everyone was eating around a table. I used my own dog "Mike," who was sitting in a chair beside me with his tail hanging down. I reached around and put his tail up on to his seat. The audience went wild. I started in "Aladdin and His Lamp" and "Brainstorm" in 1948. I started in "Anthony with Cleopatra." Then I had a lucky break.

After school, I had ballet lessons with Mrs. Dunnum for mother's sake, and voice lessons on Saturday with Mrs. Tilberton, former wife of a governor. Mother insisted I take voice lessons, because her dead mother had been known as a lady with a voice. My mother's friend Inna's daughter, Janice, was also taking voice lessons with a Mrs. Tilberton. Mrs. Tilberton had large breasts and loved bending over when I had to hit a high note. Believe me, I could hit them. Well, it worked out that Janice and I had the leads in "The Chimes of Normandy" a musical from the 18th century. This show was the first operetta my high school had ever put on. The show was a big hit. I loved all the scenery that it required— a castle and a thick forest. It was special.

Dr. Biage decided I would be great for a children's theater and we toured towns in the area with me as Jack in the Beanstalk, and was very popular with the kids.

Another after school delight was a bit confusing. The prettiest girl in our class, Joyce Lock, preferred me over other male students. It was my chance toward manhood. However, I botch it. Tim Billus often went home with me and we smooched in the basement. I'm sure that activity contributed to the "gay" bit developing in me.

Chapter 4

Thanks to my grandfather's love for my mother, he let her travel quite a lot in her youth. Then when he died he blessed her with a large inheritance. Fortunately, mother inherited land and a church. Her great grandfather had built the oak-beamed church building, when he bought out the valley called Skin Out back in the 1860s. After a church is not used for 50 years, it belongs to the owner of the land, which she inherited.

So, with some money available, she sent me to Southern University. It was the period just after WWII, when the troops were returning. Many entered the university with me. In my English class a very handsome student invited me to his apartment after class. I wondered if I would be confronted with the "game in the woods" and I was correct. Well, it had been a long time since I had played that game, so I was leery. When the host took me in his arms and kissed me, I started crying. I was too old for innocence and did not want to be known as an odd ball. I broke away, but other men soon followed. Strange, but I could not give into their wishes.

When I tried out for a play in drama class I was immediately cast in the Broadway production "Kiss and Tell" The director, Dr. McCloud, liked my performance. I was cast in many plays and was awarded best actor on campus. The cold war was on when I finished my Bachelor's Degree, so military service awaited me. I join the Air Force to escape the draft.

Chapter 5

Fanny Holland, a cute little girl I had been in school with from the first grade to High School. She was working for the government in the Post Office, sorting the papers of volunteers who were avoiding the draft. Yes, I was one of them, but how was I to know that I would return in three years having never been in an airplane. Well, in those days, everyone was moved around the country in trains. And on that train was Jack Thompson. I hadn't seen him since we were in Junior High school. He had quit school then because he could work in a WWII freight car factory and make good money. I saw him last driving a great big car. I wonder what every happened to him.

Speaking of old friends, Walter Wobst comes to mind. He was the old German guy, who I once met when I was in high school. I was attending the St. Louis opera La Traviata with my voice teacher. This was when the Metropolitan Opera was touring the country after the war. During the opera, he laughed at the right places, so we became acquainted. I invited him to my home in Mt. Vernon, and he became a friend of my family. When we would go to the opera he would make me sit with German opera Libraitoes and follow the opera from the Met. On that train to boot camp I had made arrangements for Walter to meet me at the train station. I could spend several days with him before leaving on the train for boot camp. Of course, there was more to his interest in me than music.

When my break was up Walter took me to the train station, and I caught the train to Texas. San Antonio was a delight. The Texas sun had not yet made the area so hot and I was free on weekends to leave the secret base in the hills over the metropolis. I had lots of free time. There was nothing to do. So I inquired at the general's office and they let me start a dancing school on the stage area. The General was glad that the wives of the soldiers on base wanted something for their children to do. I taught ballet and tap dancing on Saturday mornings. Turn out was great, but one little blonde girl remains in my memory, her name was Cindy. The first time we took a break from pales' and noisy taps, I asked, "What game shall we play. The darlings usually said, "Let's be butterflies." Oh what fun, but Cindy yelled, Snakes". Her mother siting up the ring of chairs around us almost stumbled over a chair. Yet Cindy surprised me every time we played the game. I figure that Cindy probably would drive a Mac truck for forty years and have a happy life.

Our stay in Texas was short and we had to close the dance school.

Chapter 6

Since my grandmother had taught me some Russian I took some test and was qualified to go to an interpreter's school at Syracuse University for eight hours a day of Russian verbs, nouns and participles. We were moved by train to Syracuse University in upstate New York. The barracks had been built at the back of the great university for us. At the train station before departure to the university, I noticed a very handsome Italian looking guy. He was truly a remnant from the Roman past. Upon arrival, we were taken immediately to the barracks. As luck would have it, he was assigned a room in the barracks that had been built for the soldiers studying the Russian language. I was Interested in meeting this Richard Bannor. I was assigned a room on the second floor, which was not far from the handsome Italian man's room. It was at that point that I realized that I wanted to know him. So, I started standing on my head with my door open when he walked down the hall in his shower clogs. Naturally he'd stop and talk. One fall day he invited me to sit on the steps at the back of our building. We took a walk into the woods behind us. Then, in the moonlight, he enfolded me in his arms. His kisses went all over my body. We were to be together for the year of Russian grammar – and romance.

Chapter 7

Companionship faded, and turned into love, a love known only by few. In the evenings we would slip out of the barracks and sit together in a wooded area. There is no way to describe Richard's body in the moonlight during our closeness. I knew then that I had wanted to be a woman all my life. We spent much time embracing our bodies. He showed me a letter he wrote to his girlfriend to break their engagement. We were planning to meet after our service and live together forever. We were simply captivated by our mutual charms. We met in bars and made plans.

Graduation time came in the early spring and a stupid clerk, not knowing our situation, sent Richard to Korea and me to Chanute Air Force base where I was the Russian Interpreter. The base was near the local University, where I would get a master's degree in Russian History. At the University I had a most wonderful experience. In my spare time I became a student of a super Russian professor, Mrs. Tricaka. She was so charming and took me under her wing. My love for Russian poetry was kindled by her. I also had Russian history with Professors Randova and Valarii. I had nothing to do in the service but study, so I did all the time. A paper I wrote for the historian received the only "A" in the class and he kept it for future students to see how well a "historical investigation" could be made.

Chapter 8

Mean while, back at the air force base, things were happening. My first roommate, Jack Mason, had arrived. He was the spoiled son of the wealthy Mason Equipment Company. He had grown up on Fifth Avenue in New York City and his grandmother was one of the sweetest little old ladies I had ever me. She had grown up on a large Louisiana Plantation with plenty of servants and fruit trees in the front yard near the Golf of Mexico. When I later met her, I was charmed by her vast understanding of the world.

Yet my second roommate, Phillip Genario, was really on the scale of the first roommate's wealth. He had been educated in Buenos Aires, where a helicopter flew him daily from the family mansion to the school across the famous River. He was also very handsome and reminded me of Richard. However, he and Jack hit it off right a way and I caught them in bed doing what married people do. It was a sight! Yet when my third roommate, Robert Bavies came, I had no desire to play bedroom with him. He was sort of an alley tramp, not good-looking and very nosy. Yes, he later proved to be quite dangerous as a tattle tail.

Chapter 9

The interpreter's wing of that huge air base had interesting people. Three of us became friends, teasing Robert about being a jerk, which was true. Still we had little work, so I opened a dance school. Yes, the governing general thought it would be good for the wives of the many common airmen. The local canteen had little music for the dance, but I had the ballet class dancing to a Strauss Waltz on the stage. Evenings were free and Jack and Phillip often took me into the crummy town for a beer. Life was fun and so were my companions. Yet we had to be very careful in those years as the police often raided gay bars. The police treated people suspected of being perverted very inhumanely. However, we also had fun in restaurants. Phillip and Jack had grown up in café society and knew how to order only the best. Phillip would often call out the chef so he could have his steak prepared just the way he liked it. I'd have settled for a wiener, but they bought me a steak too. Life was on the upscale side.

Chapter 10

It was at that time that the US Government decided to create outreach schools abroad so that students could study advanced Russian. It was impossible to study in Russia itself at that time. So I applied. I was selected as an assistant in the US Russian Program in Munich, Germany with a trip to Russia after each one. When I left Richard he swore he would remain fateful and he was glad I was to have the experience. So, I was soon flying to Munich.

Was I thrilled? Munich in the summer time was wonderful. The new opera house was open and it was spectacular. I saw Wagner's "Die Meistersinger" with its great song contest at the end. The next opera was followed by Giordano's "Andre Chérner," And Weber's "Der Freischutz." It was a glorious opera season.

At the Russian institution I immediately met members of the Old Russian aristocracy, who had fled to Munich during World War ll. The Countess von Delingshashausen invited me to dinners, because she liked to talk about their survival during the war. My stay in Germany was marvelous. On weekends I visited museums, palaces and the great countryside, hills and mountains.

Chapter 11

Then tragedy struck. Some jerk had seen Richard and me in the woods. What were they doing? You know, but air force policy did not approve in those days. I was suddenly called to the colonel's office. I did not know what to say, so I told the truth, when a lie might have saved my neck. Richard, in Korea, told the lie and was excused. I told the truth and was sent to JAIL. Yes, in those days I could not have been in a worse position. I was released from jail and sent back to America to face military discipline.

When I arrived back in America, I was called in and questioned again. As it turned out Robert Bavies was a spy and he found out from my friends about David and me in Syracuse. This reinforced the case for the Air Force legal prosecutors. Yes, a trial was held and I was found guilty because I told the truth. Why I bothered, I don't know. Once again a lie would probably have freed me. So, I was marched off to jail. Yes, prison. There is nothing like being marched off to jail. Smartass' along the way shouted ugly things at you. It was very embarrassing and humiliating, especially when you had to stop at the officer's desk, he hands you a razor and makes you take off your shirt and cut off your rank and military symbols. I would have rather cut my throat.

My friends Jack and Phillip tried to help me, but it was quite dangerous and I did not want them involved. I was sentenced at the trial as an Unfit Airman, 3rd degree (as low as possible, with a Blue Ticket discharge). It meant oblivion for me. Both friends gave me a telephone number to keep in contact. Phillip's number was in

Washington DC and Jack's to his Granny's in the Pacific Cascades. I couldn't call them. I was too embarrassed.

I was sent out in the jail's break yard, which was attached to the jail. I stood looking at the cigarette butts I was supposed to pick up. Suddenly a tall butch guy said, "What'cha you in for pal?" How does one answer that?

When I was released, I was broke and had no place to go. Shame followed me everywhere. A girl from my childhood first grade, Joann Standard, worked in the office where my papers were sent. She broke the law and told everyone I knew about my fate. What a friend she turned out to be. Kick him while he's down.

Chapter 12

The train ride back to the Chanute Air Force Base was sad and I went to pick up my things. I had to await for Air Force paper work to be completed. When I arrived there was a letter for me from an old friend at the University. His name was Michel, and he was living in San Francisco. I called him long distance and explained my situation to him. He told me to go to Western Union and wait for his reply. I went and after a couple of hours, I received a check for a hundred dollars. I was alive again. Then I was given a temporary room in the Service Quarters. It had polished floors, laundry service and food off of plates, not flat pans like in jail. The Air Force gave me an official Blue Ticket discharge and I was released from the service.

I then was able to accept a junior high school history position in the near by town of Steger, Illinois. It was a very small town that had once been the location of the Steger Piano factory. During the Depression of the 1890s it had failed and was empty. The school building was in very bad shape and the school system had very little money. However, the small $3,000 it offered was better than nothing, so I took it.

Chapter 13

In the small town of Steger there were no places where one could rent a room. A teacher at the school, a Miss Mary Pierce, loaned me her car so I could look in the neighboring town of Chicago Heights. I found a very old three-story house that had a room of sorts. The old lady that lived there said, she would bring down a huge bed from above and give me her front parlor, which was enormous. However, she forgot to tell me that her mentally ill sister would be playing cards in the kitchen. Well, I had to pass through the kitchen in order to go to the basement for a shower. On the way to the shower the frosty old sister offered me a piece of raison pie and I threw my towel around my neck to get the pie and it hit a low hanging air pipe and knocked suit down all over me. I couldn't stand the situation in the old house and had to find another place. I was told the school superintendent might have a solution and when I met his wife, Mrs. Kaltzman I was accepted into their lovely home. My living problem was solved.

Chapter 14

I had never taught school before, especially seniors. I then had the challenge of finding a way to educate seniors. So, after I started my dancing school in the basement of the building at $500 a lesson, I wrote three plays for the children to perform. They were "Indians Attacking", "A Search of the Skies" and "Farmer Family." We made scenery from old boxes left in the piano ruins. I had two students who were continually fighting with each other. I was able to convince the fat little Italian boy Warren, that it is much more gentlemanly to carry loot from the old factory than to be fighting a young, slender, fellow classmate. Together the two boys carried a ton of boards, plaster planks and stuff to the school to build an Indian village for one play, a rocket station for the second and a farmyard for the last one. We had tremendous success and Ms. Pierce helped us. That school had never before put on such a production. They offered me a permanent position. I decided that I'd better refuse and was glad I did.

Chapter 15

I got a letter from Michel that had a $100 check from his mother, Martha. She was a Brooklyn lady who new how to fight. When her husband died leaving a will that she was sure his brother had "touched", pertaining to a run of funeral establishments in Pennsylvania towns. She hired a linguist who proved the will had been changed and she won quite a settlement. Mother and son have money to burn.

Michel was the first real gay queen I ever met. He preferred sleeping with black men. His mother once called him and asked, "Your landlady say's you're sleeping with black men. Why?" Leave it to Martha to be frank and blunt. I flew to San Francisco.

Well Martha, Bless her heart, took me under her wing and took me to the California Work Bureau. The interviewer smiled and offered me a bank job typing stock certificates in the roof of the Large Bank of America. I was working for $3.50 an hour. At lest I was earning something. After three weeks of that, the lady at the Work Bureau sent me to the Pacific Gas and Electric Company. I went the next day and joined three engineers on their way to the Feather River Canyon, where I carried equipment for the workers. Once we reached the rim of the canyon the boss said, "Hey Eddie, and he pointed at me. Get an axe out of the trunk an start chopping down a path from here to there." And he pointed to the edge of the canyon.

Havening never had an axe in my hands, I choose a blunt one, and started chopping down small trees; the wrong ones of course.

Eventually I came to the canyon edge. The workers had driven to the other side and were yelling for me to raise the tall white alignment pole that they needed to start the surveying process. I had the pole, but did not understand what they were yelling about. About an hour later the truck arrived and the engineer turned the pole around. I had it up side down. This demonstrated my college background and I received a lot of teasing. They called me a "College Punk", among other things.

The next day we walked by a coiled snake, which they didn't notice. I did and yelled and pointed, "snake" out loud. They almost jumped into the canyon. After that, they were much kinder.

Then we were back in San Francisco for four days. Martha was proud of me, but Michel was too busy with his record shop. That night we went to a gay bar that had a funny show. A Christmas tree was raped by Santa Claus.

The next day we were invited to a luncheon at the apartment above us. Two dykes lived there: one VERY beautiful white girl from the South, who modeled furs for the rich in a big fashionable women's store and her friend, a black girl who sang in a nightclub. Both girls fell for each other in high school because Olivia felt sorry for the way Sally was treated. It was a merry group, but of course, Michel got drunk and said he could do a summersault. He knocked over a large vase of green vermouth on a white rug. Then he decided to jump into his convertible car on a Frisco hill and cut his foot. We all proceeded to the hospital.

Chapter 16

Four days passed and I met the truck at the canyon. I was put on a different team. It seems the big cheese thought I didn't understand such work. I wonder why?

My new boss was just the opposite of my other boss the old fart. Mr. Matson thought I was unique. I was a student to be at a large University in Illinois. He realized how difficult that was and liked me. For instance, one morning he met us in the parlor of our hotel and said, "Let's not work today. Mr. Evans hasn't seen Mt. Shasta, so let's show him." So, we spent the day going up into the Feather River Forest. Wow, the views were amazing. That man was just a wonderful human being. Even the whores he took to bed were pleasant. I'll never forget his kindness. He even asked me to sing ballads occasionally. Not the trash that was popular at the time. Wish I knew his fate.

The Three Rivers National Forest was fascinating. Glorious trees, valleys and streams everywhere. We stayed in a woodman's cabin and the host was the chef. At the first dinner I took a napkin from a glass in the middle of the table. The second I touched the napkin; I knew no one had ever taken one before. All the men saw me and laughed, but no one called me college punk.

Chapter 17

The summer came to an end and I was back in wicked San Francisco. Jeb, A friend of Homer De Homas had a marvelous apartment that stretched over a hill that allowed a view of both big bridges—Golden Gate and the big city one. Jeb's parties were always great. His white pools had won many blue ribbons. He told me that if I'd stay and not return to the Midwest, he'd teach me hair-bunting and let me work in his beauty shop. I was tempted, since I wasn't sure about the future. Michel's offer still sounded good too. Still, I decided that both offers expected more of me than I wanted to give. So I turned them down.

It just so happened that a bit of luck came my way. An old college friend named Fannie, showed up at Michel's. She was pregnant and planning to drive back to the Mid-West. She asked if I could go with her to help with the driving. The man who had given her a baby gave her $3,000 cash to have the baby elsewhere. He was a wealthy lawyer and didn't want her or the baby. In the meantime we drove from San Francisco to a shady spot in Nevada. We ate sour pickles there and drove on. In St. Louis Fannie was blessed with a boy at her friend's house. When Fannie gave birth she had a picture of his son placed in the front window of his lawyer father's office. I then had another streak of luck.

Chapter 18

At Steger, the school that couldn't afford a fart, a dear Mrs. Meade taught. She liked me and told her husband about me. He was Dr. Meade, the head of another government program that was bringing 40 Indian engineers to America to study Steel Technics. All I had to do was see that they got on the bus in the mornings. We all lived in the large international house of the University. While they went to the Steel mill, I took courses at the University.

When the Indians arrived, there was an immediate problem. The cleaning lady at the international house told me that the Indians were leaving their bowel movements on the cover of the stools. "What is going on?" she asked me. Well, one of the Indians named Gopal, was quite Western. His father had put him in Japanese Universities and then New York University. So, he joined the Indian group already aware of American ways. I asked him about the problem and he said that the men were untouchables, so they could not sit on the top of the stools. They had to hang out over the stool and let go. Plus, they could not clean up their own mess. He helped me convince them that In America it's all right to sit on the stools and crap in the stool.

Chapter 19

So, began a friendship that was to be most wonderful and a real savior for me. Gopal and I became close friends. We seemed destine to have qualities that bound us together. Those aspects first showed the evening we won a card contest in the main salon of the International house. He played much better than I did, but for some reason I was there with the right cards when he needed them. After wining, we thanked our fellow travelers for their congrats and went to the elevator. In the hall he followed me to my room. We were standing by the extra bed when he pulled me down on it and began embracing me. I gave into his rapture and we stayed together all night. Our togetherness was sealed. Our romance was real.

Fellow Indians gradually caught on to our feelings and thought nothing of it. In India it was not uncommon for two men to have a romantic attachment for each other. Gopal even began calling me Sumdar Bonder, in Hindi, which means beautiful monkey in English. Life could not have been sweeter. Yet it became so. Gopal bought me a new car, a Chevrolet. My comrades wanted a ride, so I made several trips with several small groups to fine hotels to give them the pleasure of "the American lifestyle". They loved it.

Fortunately, Gopal could afford to take me to the best restaurants. His father owned industries in India and would send him what he needed. We lived a high life overlooking the skyscrapers, while we dined in fancy restaurants. If only it had not ended!

The year at the University International House did end and Gopal was expected to return home after all the years in foreign universities. Our plan was for us two to drive out to Los Angels in my car. There we would part. I was set to teach history in a High School in Long Beach, California and he was to return home. Imagine my surprise when he told me that he was arranging for me go to India. Whoopee! I would teach a half-year while he made arrangements for me to come to India. When I took him to the airport for his return. We embraced in the tunnel he took to his plane. I watched him fly away in to the evening sunset. I was now alone again.

Chapter 20

Fortunately I was able to rent a small side room to a house not far from a Local High School. I decorated the classroom with short phrases in the various languages I knew— Chinese, Hindi, Russian and English. I thought it would inspire students to study. Wrong! I did not have a good understanding of students at that time In California. Classes were broken into capabilities— above average students, average students and below average students. I thought it a rather unfair system, but enjoyed teaching the first group.

On the first day of school that fall, the principal asked me for a brief chat. He told me that I was to receive a problem boy in my lower level class. I felt that it meant that he had tried all the other teachers in the school and was now trying me. So, I saved a seat by my desk for the arrival of Marvin, who never showed up. As I was talking with the students when classes started, I noticed something sort of pop up and down in the last row. I walked back there and saw a little boy eating popcorn out of his pockets. "Hi, Doc." he said as I approached. I took him by the collar and walked him up to the desk I had saved for him. So began my efforts to make a human out of a you-name-it student. The class began reading in their history book, but I noticed that Marvin's book was up side down. I called and asked him to read the book aloud and he said, out loud, "tion!" I said "What?" and he repeated "tion!" I looked and the page had its last syllable on the next page. So began my adventures with Marvin.

The most incredible experience that I remember was when a frog sound resounded in the room. I turned to Marvin and said, "Marvin don't do that." He answered, "It wasn't me." I said to him, "You know the punishment if you do it again. You have to go to the Principle's office." The windows in this California schoolroom went from ceiling to the floor. Suddenly a student yelled, "Hey, there's a frog in here." I looked quickly and found that there was a frog. A real frog was in the base of the window. I couldn't help but laugh. A little later I mentioned the name "Algeria," while we were studying Civics. Marvin asked about it and I said, "We aren't studying Algeria, We're studying German Nationalism. The next day he brought several books from the library about Algeria to the class. I let him read them, while we talked about Nationalism. That continued for several days. Finally the course ended and Marvin had made an "F" on every exam, so he had failed. Later he came in the room and asked, "But what about Algeria?"

To this very day I have regretted that I did not give him at least a "D" for Algeria! He could have stayed in school. What would it have mattered? He had actually taken an interest in something. Forgive me Marvin, wherever you are.

I have never heard the word "Algeria" without thinking of little Marvin. Even when I was later in Algeria, I kept hoping I'd run into him. One day in the Kasbah market, I heard someone yell, "Marvin". I turned, but did not see him. I did think of a line he repeated —"My father always tells me to go play on the Freeway! The poor kid must have had a terrible life!

Chapter 21

Fortunately for me, the end of the school year happened just in time for Gopal to come for me. He did and we were soon flying over the ocean to India via Honolulu, Japan, Hong Kong and Burma. I was then in the country of my dearest friend and it was to become the wonder of my life. Never had I seen such crowded streets, such unusual clothing and such lavish hotels. We stayed in a famous new hotel in New Delhi named "The Ashoka". From the balcony of our room I could see a nearby field. I asked Gopal what was moving around in that field. He looked and said, "That's where people are living. They are living in mud cottages. It was the beginning of my discovery of the "other world" I didn't know.

Just imagine the huge British Arch Way in Bombay that has welcomed foreigners into the mystical and fantastic world of India, ever since the English conquered the country. It is a magnificent structure and well designed to fit the glories ahead. So Gopal and I left the airport and boarded a small boat to the great Arch. I was actually in India and Gopal was determined to show me his country as I had shown him some of mine.

Gopal was eager to go to his home in Agra, so we took a taxi to anther airport for a flight to the city of the Taj Ma Hal. He told me that he would not let me see the famous building until we could see it in moonlight, so we immediately went to his home when we landed in Agra.

After meeting his mother, I was taken to the breakfast room. It was there that I made my first mistake. On the wall was a large picture of an ancient Goddess. She was holding what looked like something she might be selling. I asked, "What is she selling?" Gopal immediately started laughing and explained to the two businessmen, who were also guests. It was a Hindu goddess. I apologized, but Gopal enjoyed my error.

I had much to learn, for instance, don't go walking without something in your hand to throw at a monkey. They won't bother you that way, but without out something in your hand you might be ganged up on and lose your purse or pride. Yes, monkeys were in abundance in Agra where we lived. The rooms were spread out from one another, so Gopal paid servants to live on the roof of the rooms to handle the monkey problem.

We flew to Calcutta to visit with Gopal's father in a large three-floored castle-like building where we ate on a third floor pavilion. The kitchen was on the roof so meals would go upward. Gopal's father told us that he had ordered "water balls" for dinner. At the table were small bowls by each plate filled with a greenish liquid. I watched to see what everyone did with the balls. They took a small dough ball out of a center container. Then they filled it with the greenish liquid and put it in their mouth. It was one of those times when you couldn't swallow or spit it out. To be sociable I swallowed, and I still remember the burn on my tongue. The burn went all the way down to my little toe.

I soon learned to eat the many dishes that were prepared for me and learned to love Indian food.

Fortunately, Gopal had planned a trip to his many factories. I was taken along— either by plane, train or coach. Yes, I saw India from the top (Kashmir) to the bottom (Mahabaleshwar). In Agra, we lived within a mile from the incredible Taj Ma Hal. It's majesty is one of the world's wonders and Gopal took me to see it first in the moonlight it was almost transparent in that light.

Chapter 22

My year in India was filled with the great palaces, temples and historical places that made Gopal so proud and eager for me to see as much as possible. When I left, I signed a paper for him that noted that I was an "industrial expert". Yes, he used me as a deduction on his income tax and I was glad he did. I had seen and lived a year in fabulous India. No place had been too far to travel. He sent me to the high peeks of the world. The Himalayans is where I slept in a sheepherder's mound of dead plants and on a houseboat on Lake Shalimar. Famous battle scenes like Fatehpur Sikri fascinated me. He took me to a little chemical clinic where he was doing some experiments. I went up on its roof and to my amazement; the Taj Ma Hal was way across a field there. I told him he should build a hotel there, but he said that the bridge over the river before the Taj was too far away. A hotel would not be practical.

Well, when we drove to Madras in the South of the country, he wanted to see a factory he was building. I asked, "What's that over there." He replied, another factory being built by the government, but they are so slow my factory will be running for five years before they finish. He laughed. I saw where Buddha sat under the tree for knowledge all those centuries ago. I saw people lying by the Ganges River. I asked what they were doing. Gopal said "They are killing themselves so they can go directly to being Brahmin in the next life. Gopal truly gave me an amazing tour of India. Then I headed back to America.

Chapter 23

On the flight back east I had three hamburgers before I landed in the big city. I went to the International House for lunch and memories. Was it possible that Gopal was not there to take me on a walk through the old architecture of the center section of the University? It had always been my favorite place. Yet in a sense he was with me and we sat down on a stone bench that I loved. Life had been good to me and India was now a glorious part of my past.

Chapter 24

Lake Forest, Illinois

Since I had been accepted to teach Russian at Lake Forest University, I went to the small campus and met the dean. He explained that the faculty was on a short holiday at a resort not far away, and that he would take me there that afternoon. First he drove me around Lake Forest, a very beautiful area where one doesn't see roofs, mainly just high chimneys. Which is an indication that a billionaire lived there in his mansion. The town was famous for having once been the home of more millionaires than any other place in America. I was impressed.

At the resort Lake in Wisconsin I met members of the faculty. One guy named John, a teacher of Psychology, seemed to pay me much attention. Since he was to be my roommate, I allowed him to take me home at the end of the three days. He had one of the apartments built for faculty. So we divided the available drawers and I moved in. How was I to know that he had a mad desire for me that is, in bed. I found out once when one of my students came to me and asked if she could ask some personal questions. I agree and she said that she was planning to marry my roommate John. I knew she had relatives in Lake Forest, which meant money. I could hardly believe that he would be interested in her financial situation, because he had a wealthy grandmother in Oklahoma.

When he asked me to move so he could give her my bed, I was distraught. Move to where? That night I let him have me and

I assumed he'd let me stay. Wrong. He merely wanted to get me out of the way. Did they marry? To this day I don't know, because I transferred back to the International House at the University in Chicago. I did see her once more and advised her not to trust him. I guess I shouldn't have.

Chapter 25

It seemed wonderful to be back at the International House, where I had met Gopal. However, I was not to stay there for a long time. A unique experience came my way. The University of Texas was in great need of a Russian Professor. I was offered the position in a most advantages manner. Since I was scheduled to report to the University of Texas in a few days, I went back to the big city and check In with the University to make sure that all was finished with my transfer to Texas. That University of Texas was so in need of professors of Russian, it had offered me a unique program. I would teach an advanced course and also be given time to work on my dissertation for back in the big city University. After talking with the dean of Humanities, I was shown my office, which I was to share with another professor, Tamara Fedorovana. She and I immediately stopped talking English and began speaking in Russian. She had a very sophisticated pronunciation. It was aristocratic and very impressive, and so was her background.

Tamara's father had been a student in the last class of the Corps des Pages of the last Tsar of Russia, Nicholas the II. Her mother was from the Zarzhadsa clan in Gruszia (Georgia), who were the kings of that country in the 14th century. A more aristocratic background could not have been imagined. However, she did not want to brag. She would say, "You are born an aristocratic and there's nothing you can do about it." Still, I envied her exclusive background and slowly developed her accent. A close friendship immediately developed. That evening after the first meeting of the Russian Club, where we met our students. We walked home hand in hand.

Chapter 26

My friend Gopal in India had joined one of his factories with Corning Glass Company in New York State. Since he made money for that company, they occasionally brought him to America. He would ask them to schedule his itinerary through the place I would be, and we were able to visit. Tamara and I took Gopal to a fancy Mexican restaurant. That evening Gopal said, "Eddie, that woman wants to marry you. Why don't you? I don't mind because we see each other rarely now." It was food for thought, and I couldn't resist her intelligence and background.

Tamara and I married within three months, and our ceremony was accidental. In the state I was raised in one had to wait three days before they could marry. In Texas that wasn't true. So when we went for the certificate, the clerk asked, "Are you now going upstairs and be married?" The bride and groom looked at each other and nodded "Yes." We went upstairs and married and then went to her apartment and called our parents. My parents were delighted. Tamara's mother was kind, then said, "I am going to fly to see you. Please meet my plane. I met her plane and found out the reason for the hurry. She wanted a private talk with me. She then asked me if Tamara had told me about her illness. I told her that Tamara had told me briefly, but she didn't go into detail. I was shocked to find out that the illness was schizophrenia. Her mother then told me that she had spent her life trying to find a cure for her daughter. She also added that she would never hold it against me if I wanted to divorce her now. I was flabbergasted. I did not know all the consequences from her past. I told her mother that we were in love, and would face the consequences together. We stayed married.

When I was transferred to the University in California, Tamara's mother, Mrs. Techevskia moved to Corona Del Mar, a beautiful grotto on the coast of Southern California. She wanted to help me with my wife. I discovered very quickly what she meant by the word "help." While driving 65 miles an hour from Los Angeles on the eight lane Highway Five, Tamara suddenly tried to open the car door on her side. I had to reach over and grab her, pull her back into the car, watch the traffic on both sides of the car, and pulled over to the curb when I could. It was quite an introduction to a wife's problem. One could not really be sure when she was suddenly very nervous, but one learned to watch for indications.

A more common indication of her anxiety could be in the night when a wee small voice would say, "You aren't sleeping." If I had to lecture the next day, I would beg her to let me sleep. I never knew exactly why she would want to bother me, but it caused me to feel uneasy later before an audience. Her mother understood her better and sympathized with me when such incidents occurred. We did not rebuke her for her disturbances, but waited patiently for it to pass. Such things also occurred in the mornings. One never knew what kind of reaction the experience might be for her. She could be such a loving sweet person or a withdrawn soul seeking understanding or help.

Chapter 27

Southern California was not for Tamara and me. We did not grow up with an ocean nearby, so a beach did not seem a happy place for a party. We would be invited to spend the day there, but always left as soon as possible. Having been reared in a small town, driving the long distance back to Irvine was nerve racking. Especially when I had to keep an eye out for any problem I could see in Tamara on the way back. When an offer from a large University near Washington D.C. arrived, we decided to go back East. The University in California had been very good to me and advised me not to leave, but for Tamara's health, it seemed best to go where we did have many friends.

Driving through my home state gave us the chance to visit my parents and my brother John and his wife, Rosemary, who lived in a small town close by. The first stop was most delightful, as my parents were delighted to welcome us. They had spent a week with us in California, but had also witnessed one of Tamara's spells. It had been very sad and my mother and father were eager to do everything possible to keep a calm atmosphere. My father was an amateur fine artist. He had little training, but his paintings were quite impressive. He showed Tamara some of his paintings and interested her in his art. During the depression of the 1930's he had painted portraits for people that wanted a memory picture of a relative. One picture he was painting of a farmyard for a widow friend, caused my mother to say, "Edwin, you obviously did not grow up on a farm. You've made all the chickens into roosters. Oh, those poor hens." Dad had made roosters because their feathers were more colorful. He changed some back to hens. Even Tamara was amused.

The fun of being with family ceased when we went to my brother's home. There had been uneasiness in his marriage ever since he had married Rosemary. She was a sickly girl who was a neighbor in our youth. Rosemary hated mother because she knew that Mother did not want her son to marry her. It did condemn my brother to 60 years of hospitals, doctors and medical experts. Also, in her psychic ways, Rosemary turned my brother John into a mound of putty, which she could mold into a very unhappy human being. We stayed only one evening with that unhappy couple.

Chapter 28

When we arrived at the University home town, old friends of my mother-in-law welcomed us immediately. Mr. and Mrs. Frank Flowers of Woodbury, New Jersey had us up for a week on their private lake. Tamara seemed in better health than any time before. We were glad we had made the move. Then, Mr. & Mrs. Malvor invited us to Charlestown, Virginia where they wanted me to transfer to the University by them so we could be in close proximity. I told them I couldn't right now, but would think about it in the future. Another close friend, Elizabeth Lucas called us from Philadelphia and said she was coming for a visit. She had been Tamara's girlfriend since the 3rd grade at the Friends school in New York. We were delighted to hear from her. Our friends were making life very comfortable. We couldn't imagine what could go wrong?

Wrong? Well, while old friends had certainly welcomed us at my new University, I was to meet the saddest human being I had ever had the displeasure of meeting. He was head of the University's Russian Department, Dr. Donald Handcock. He had been a handsome man in his youth and he had an enviable education at Yale, with the world's most famous Slavistische. The Nazis had forced them out of Europe and together at Yale they were known for their books and research as a formidable force.

My own efforts paled in comparison, but I never even tried to translate ancient Slavic texts. It wasn't my area of study. Of course, it brought him much attention. When I graduated with my masters, I only had one course in Old Church Slavonic and it was taught by the daughter of one of the famous ones. She was a Chizevsky, which brought angels from above and bouquets in circles around her. There was however, a rumor that the old genius kept her in chains in their basement, while she translated. Heaven knows she knew nothing about teaching. She was noted for calling a student by the error he had made in translation. I was Mr. Genetive Pural for two weeks because I slipped once and thought I was correct, I was in a small class of seven students, one lady maintained that her monthly period went haywire from the pressure given us by that monster from the depths. We students went to a bar after class and cried about the madness she was teaching. All of us suffered except for one boy whom we all hated. Chezevsky would leave the door open if precious was late. Then she would ask how the baby was. We doubted that he had one. Can you imagine our delight when we learned that he was gay. I laughed until I cried. Remembering those days always gives me a laugh.

Chapter 29

Back to my teaching job. Well, you had to give Handcock credit. After all he had survived being a student of such a powerhouse. Yet he was noted for doing nothing. I can still see him sitting by his desk waiting for an inspiration. I guessed that was what he was doing. Nothing else seemed to make sense. The one thing I did not like about his teaching was that, he included his students in his private affairs. That is, if a student asked about his mother's health, he would go into detail about his problems in taking care of her. Heavens, my wife Tamara was much more of a problem than his mother, but I never mentioned what I had at home. Handcock seemed to like such attention.

Some things are evident in his career. He never did anything for the purpose of promoting the department's reputation. I gave speeches in seven national Slavic conferences and two in International meetings by invitation of the leaders. I spoke at the conference at Banff, Canada and the International Conference in London, I was praised for each presentation about Dostoevsky.

Handcock was also greatly rebuffed, when he tried to sue our department head for saying that he did little professionally. I found the trial most amusing, because he had nothing to support his own estimate of himself. Letters from Slavisists all around the world came, and wrote negatively about him. He lowered his price from 100 to nothing, but still failed. One could not help but be amused.

Chapter 30

The Dean of Humanities asked professors to write their opinion of their department head. I wrote what I thought of Professor Metier of the German Depart. To my horror, the Dean gave my letter to Professor Metier. It caused the department head to take vengeance on me.

The Dean of Humanities, Professor Eisenaven decided to prove that I was an anti-semite. He hired a young Slavisist, Dr. John Tadd, to carry out his plan against me. Mr. Tadd was a Professor at the University of Indiana and was eager to advance himself. When he came to the University, he immediately invited my wife and me to dinner. That evening he spoke most unkindly of Jews and bragged about growing up in a home where his father hated Jews. Tamara and I were flabbergasted at his conduct and thought it strange that Mr. Tadd spoke so unkindly about Israel. He also began bringing visiting Slavisists to my home and continued his condemnation of the Jewish minority. Since there is nothing in my background that would make me an anti-Semite, I did not participate in Mr. Tadd's campaign to smear me.

To my great surprise, Professor Tadd was chosen to help in clearing the Russian town of Chernobyl, where the failed nuclear power plant had destroyed much property, and filled the area with radiation poisoning. Mr. Tadd, was eager for the attention the trip would make for him. He did go to Chernobyl, where he caught lung cancer from the radiation. He asked me to attend his funeral, but

I refused because of his ridiculous efforts to prove prejudice about my character.

I had worked enough time to retire from the University. I was glad to get away from all the drama. I decided that for Tamara's health and my displeasure with the Dean's disgusting self-centeredness, I would retire. After I retired, I was offered several lecture tours on high-end cruise lines. I spent the next twenty years lecturing for Renaissance, Regent, Silver Sea and other cruises lines.

Chapter 31

I was lucky to find a friend while on one of my cruises. We met him once, while my mother-in-law Laskia and I played Russian Scrabble on the ship deck as passengers walked by. The game brought us attention and Glen once joined the visitors at our table. He became a friend and was glad to join me on other cruises so I wouldn't have to go alone. He lived in Indiana, and often visited us at our home as well as on the cruises. He became so close he was like a "relative" we could depend on.

Unfortunately, after several cruises my wonderful Mother-in-law, Mrs. Laskia Federorovina passed away during her treatment for cancer. It was a tremendous loss for me, since she always helped me when Tamara would be suffering an attack of schizophrenia. We deposited Laskia's ashes in the family mausoleum in Philadelphia.

My wife took her mother's death very hard, and began to withdraw from the world. She started to become ill whenever we took a lecture cruise. Consequently she chose to stay in a clinic-hotel in Virginia, while I continued lecturing on the cruise ships. A great sadness befell me. Tamara's illness got steadily worse. Several years later she suffered a heart attack and her ashes were deposited next to her mothers in the Mausoleum.

After she was gone, I was lonely and looking for some way to keep me occupied. I decided to take art lessons from a Russian friend we had in Baltimore. Her name was Nina Radonovsky. She was a famous artist in Baltimore and worked for the Art Museum.

I became fascinated with her and her background. Even though she was older, we fell in love and I married her.

Laskia and Nina gave me the opportunity of judging the Russian Revolution of 1917 in two ways. Laskia was from the Zarzhaze, an aristocracy dating back to the 13th century in Grusia (Georgia). Where as, Nina was from the landowning gentry, whose father was a white night in the Czars army. The difference between the two social groups was astounding and fascinating. For a student of Russian History I was certainly in position to understand the reactions and discipline of the two groups during the famous Russia Revolution.

Nina and I had six years together before she perished with a heart failure. She was an amazing addition to my life of harassment.

Cruises with
Dr. Edward T. Evans
as Lecturer

1. 1999— Helsinki & St. Petersburg with Imperial Russian Historical Society of Canada

2. 2000— Crimea and Moscow with Russian Historical Society of Canada

3. 2006— China and Tibet with Viking Lines, May and June

4. Caribbean with Princess Cruises

5. Hawaii with Princess Cruses.

6. Jordan, Syria & Egypt

7. Footprints of St Paul with voyages Jules Verne & Black Sea

8. Viet Nam on the Emerald

9. Moscow —Volga River

10. Caribbean with Noble Caledonia- Moscow to Astrakhan

11. Caribbean with Celebrity Cruises

12. Volga River from Moscow to St. 'Petersburg.

13. Rage to Berlin with Viking Cruises

14. Around Great Britain with Regent Cruises

15. Around South America with Silver Sea Cruises

16. Croatia and Bulgaria River Cruises

17. Burma with Viking Cruise Lines

18. Cuba with Holland America Veendam

After retirement from his University Russian Department, Dr. Evans lectured 22 times in the Adult Program of a Baltimore University. He set a record in that program, while also lecturing on board cruise ships.

Dr. Evans also did many lectures at the Smithsonian Institute

Printed in the United States
by Baker & Taylor Publisher Services